THE BIG CROCODILE

A Song by
Ethel Crowninshield

Illustrated by
Elwood H. Smith

CELEBRATION PRESS
Pearson Learning Group

The crocodile is fast asleep.
Shhh, shhh.

On tip-toe through the grass
we'll creep. Shhh, shhh.

His great big mouth
he opens wide. Shhh, shhh.

Oh, see his sharp white teeth
inside. Shhh, shhh.

We'll leave him lying in the sun.
Shhh, shhh.

His legs are short and he can't run.
Shhh, shhh.

The crocodile is fast asleep.
Shhh, shhh.